Now
and
Then

Now
and
Then

Poems and Songs
A Random Selection
1979-2019

Zomala Abell

Book cover and interior design by Zomala Abell
and Bo von Hohenlohe Productions
Music transcription James Marchand
musicjrm@aol.com
Back cover photo by Rebecca Johnson
www.rebeccajohnsonart.com
Book production by Bo von Hohenlohe Productions
www.bvhprods.com

ISBN-13: 978-0-578-59297-8
ISBN-10: 0-578-59297-5

Library of Congress Control Number: 2019917083

Zomala Abell
Educational Explorations
PO Box 915
Albion, California 95410

This Book Is Dedicated To

Everyone I love, everyone who loves me, everyone I like, everyone who likes me, everyone I have ever seen or who has seen me, everyone I have ever read about, everyone I have never thought about, family, friends, acquaintances, strangers, 2 legged, 4 legged, many legged and no legged, gilled and winged, all living beings, including the rocks and the stars.

May all beings live with freedom, kindness, peace and joy.

Postscript: A special dollop of appreciation to my children, grandchildren, friends, and all my teachers.

Introduction and or Extroduction
...as you prefer...

One purpose of writing this book was to get rid of the piles of journals under my desk, under my bed, under my couches and filling more than one whole bookcase in a small house. The journals were written one a month, most months for about forty years. I stopped writing them about five years ago. I did not want them to be here for my kids to clean up, never mind read. I, also, didn't want to just throw them out, because I wanted the poems that I had written in them.

I have always written. Writing was, and is, an essential part of my daily practice. Through the years I have made lists with friends called, "titles of as yet unwritten books". Now, because of wanting to deal with the journals, because I want to gift myself, my community, and the world, and because I am about to turn eighty years old, "Yes," I thought, "I will finally write a book!"

The process of searching through pages and pages of journals and ripping out nuggets of poems was an adventure itself. I hadn't written those journals making meaningful and intelligent connections with world events. I had written them for myself about how I was feeling emotionally or physically or spiritually at that daily life moment. It turns out that day after day, year after year, me getting in touch with myself was very helpful in terms of becoming friends with myself. The repetition of my emotional life, however, I found boring. The rediscovery of the poetry was satisfying, stimulating, fascinating, meaningful and inspiring.

The other thing I found searching the journals, was that the poems were in fact, nuggets. They were the beginnings of poems, or the middle, or a powerful image, or a great idea. They had been written in a context where everything else was more important. They had squeezed themselves into the journals because they had insisted on coming into my life. I had not had a minute to edit, complete, or polish them. Meanwhile, I now had a big pile of torn out pages, and still had the goal of writing a book of poetry.

To actually create this book I had to learn to finish a piece of work. I love spontaneous creativity, which is what I had experienced all those years. This more complex aspect of the creative process is a deepening, difficult and exciting learning for me. These poems have been quietly ruminating, all these years, through every and all events of my life. The act of writing words has been an illumination for me through every joyful, transcendent, and devastating aspect of being alive. I feel satisfied and grateful that these words are now whole pieces, here to bear witness to themselves and to the persistence of creative energy itself.

Most of the poems in this book have been through quadrillions of versions. Sometimes the nugget is still the strongest force, sometimes is has gone away altogether. I have not always found that one version is "better" than another. I am one of those poets who, on my deathbed will be deliberating whether the word "the" or "a" is the absolutely correct choice for that particular line. The songs and chants are from prayer rituals.

What else? I would love for someone, you, to be transformed by this book. I will, however, be extremely delighted if you are simply touched by one poem. I would also like a meditation teacher to read a poem of mine at a retreat. Again, I am not fussy, it can be a meditation teacher who only teaches one time. Poems are like the leaves on a tree, you can hold one and look carefully and be exalted and unified with the world. On the other hand, there they all are with each other, and they fall in the autumn, and the tree is really the important aspect, isn't it? Poems, by their very nature, appear dispensable. There is also fame and fortune to be sought after. I will get to that, maybe.

Oh, I almost forgot. The "I" in many poems is not necessarily me. I hope that sometimes you will find that it is you.

Contents

Contents

A Blank Page

I could write a poem of a blank page
You could bring your sorrow and find solace
You could bring your joy and find sharing in celebration
You could write your story in invisible ink
All the way to the bottom of my page
And that would be a happy ending

Here We Are

Here we are
This multicolored mind
This loopity loop ride
Scratchy seats
Sharp metal safety belts
The cajoling and commanding
Invitation to win
Is so loud we can hear it
Over the continuous clatter and whirr
Of motors thumping in imitation
Of the heart of the earth
The wheels of the ride car scream with us
Around each corner
As we rise and fall
In the glued, nailed, riveted and painted
Imagined and fleshed
Ticky tacky
Neon lights spinning
Here for this holiday weekend only
Carnival of life.

Alone

The angels are loud this morning
This is how it is
This noisy universe
Silence sings
Space dances
I cannot really be alone

Though I play ragged parts
Though I wrap myself in thought
The true story is in my blood
I cannot escape
This incessant pulse
This joy

Imperfection

"There's imperfection in this perfect world.."

The melody is the silk blue sky
Sweeping white clouds
And a taste...

Salt on my tongue
As I step out of the ocean...

I know I'll go right back
Into that dark vast birthing water
Because the heat...

Sulfur yellow, orange flame tips
Burn as I scramble
Digging toes down into cooler sand
Like a frenzied crab
I crawl onto shaded aqua towel

All the people on this beach
All the voices...
All the voices are singing
This same catchy tune

"There's imperfection in this perfect world"

Little kids red suited
Jump, tumble, shout and splash
In the cool shallow whoosh along the shore

My eyes squint in the shimmering brilliance
My quick tangy breaths
Heave in and out
Adding my rhythmic life whisper
To this glorious crescendo

"There's imperfection in this perfect world"

The Gods Are Only Human

The gods are only human you know
the gods are only human you know
so for a good start
take a path with heart
and play your part

The Gods Are Only Human

The Gods are on - ly hu - man you know. The Gods are on - ly hu - man you know. so for a good start take a path with heart and play your part.

Fragment

sometimes...
all i have to offer
is a fragment

how could I eat the whole
dark 70% cocoa with bits of ginger
while imagining handing it to you ?

what was i thinking ?
i was thinking
that if i dared
i would share the chocolate right then
right there on the bus
with the smiling guy in the next seat

i didn't dare...
that's how i am sometimes

i do dare now
to offer you
the wrinkled wrapping
that still smells of sweetness

because i love you so much
but maybe it's because
you love me so much ?

sometimes... i just don't know...

now i'm thinking
maybe a fragment is enough

maybe the whole candy bar is a fragment
that guy could have been you
you could be a fragment of god ?

i don't know...
but sometimes…
that's what i think

Ashes

Almost touching hands
Almost touching hips
We are comforted by the thin blanket of space between us
And the many sure days of time since our last kiss
We sit on the white couch
Our feet are on the straw mat of the floor
You are wrapped in echo memories
I am clothed in empty skin of loss
The gentle air is aching to embrace us
But it doesn't dare to touch
Such delicate cocoons of ash
The circulation in our feet
Is slowed by blame
The bones of our hands
Are paralyzed by struggle and desire
We sit in perfect discord
A salvo to the illusion of consummation, separation and despair
Neither of us can see
That the white walls of the room remain firm
In witness to the truth
That this blessed love remains exalted and untouched.

Kaleidoscope

My heart is called broken
You are called friend
The telephone may be a wall
A wall can be a window
A flower was known as a word
A bouquet of flowers from a friend
When it is sitting by the wall
Opens the window
To mending my day
I receive your bouquet
In full aroma
In full color
I place all the flowers
Cut stems still wet with severance
In a clear glass vase
In front of the open window
As if the nights and days are orderly
And at ease in the service of life.

Rootbound

Spike leaves spike
talk bristle my caution
potted plant root tendrils
fifty years twining.
You touched
the body that I was.
She touched
the body that I was.
I want everything back
that ever happened.
Minerals in the soil
growth in the stillness
and water
water to shine my green.

Shaken

this is the season
of waiting for rain
each leaf quiet
and well behaved
like a child alone
listening for a footfall
withering with need
this is the time
for a downpour
a cascade
of water so fast falling
so full of the power of glee
it shakes the very life stem
of each leaf
and feeds the very roots
of that child
with a strength
that appears to be
freedom from need

There Are No Demons

There are no demons outside the mind
the snake about to strike
can peacefully unwind
through the dark tunnels of the night
basking in the warm sunlight

There Are No Demons

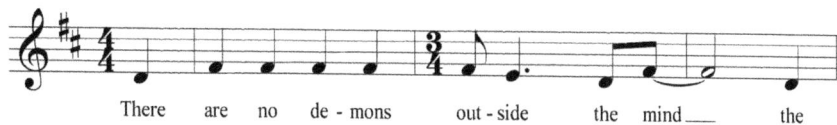

There are no de-mons out-side the mind___ the

snake a-bout to strike can peace-ful-ly un - wind

through the dark tun - nels___ of the night

bask - ing in the warm sun - light

Days of Life

The days of life are short,
unless you are waiting
for the sirens to stop.
Today on the telephone
I spoke with my sister,
my sister,
who somehow lived through the last year of war.

"This time," my sister said, "there are no labels on the bombs.
The whole world is attacking us,
I wave my passport to the sky. No one cares."

"What do you mean?" I said, "I am writing to the government
right now. It's unseasonably hot and humid here,
we are going swimming when I finish writing."

"The pages of my passport are burning," she said,
"where the gas pipe broke, along with the blankets you sent,
the fire keeps us warm.
There is no government to receive your letter,
I barely exist to be speaking with you."

"What do you mean?" I said, "You survived last time. You will
live, I'll find a way to bring you here."

"No," she said. There was static on the phone.
"There are no airplanes without bombs,
there is no fuel, except for tanks,
and really, I no longer want to come."

"No," I said, "I'll send new blankets,
I'll send a package today with canned soup and a can opener,
I'll send dried figs and apples, I'll send flour and sugar,
you'll get stronger and then when the ticket arrives you'll come.
We have beds and ice cream, we have newspapers and music,
we have toothbrushes and a dog."

"No," she said, "the children will not leave home.
The children are not interested in anything except crying,
they play at who cries loudest, who cries softest,
they drink the tears.
All day they pretend to be asleep
all night they gaze at the sky,
they can no longer leave home."

"Oh, please," I said, "oh, please!"
The phone crackled and sputtered.
"Oh, please, I'll send bicycles and dolls
the children will learn new games
everyone will have a new home.
I'll send names and addresses.
You'll fly and you'll wake up here."

"No," she said, "I am not crazy,
you wake up.
I am telling you the truth.
There are no names on the bombs.
There is no home that is not part of this war."

Beyond Blessings

beyond blessings that comfort my body
in goose feathers of warmth
beyond the sheer joy of sliding belly to belly
into sweet passion of darkness
beyond a misty rainbow dampening babies
giggling in safe green backyards
beyond a winning catch smack into the mitt
leap in smiling delight, exhale into the one air we all breath
beyond the daily and special blessing
of the sun rising and setting
a swooping mama swallow dabbing mud on her chirping nest
the meandering tumble of a multi-yellow speckled autumn leaf

beyond our concrete and steel city
twinkling with all flavors of being alive
beyond our inviting porch light small town
neighborhood at dusk
beyond our forest that honors each footstep with softness

are junkyards of endless rows of bulky overfilled storage units
gaping moldy refrigerators, broken red plastic toys
rusted piles of crushed cars
here in a vast and bleak landscape of ponderous shapes
dead roots entangle and hump up out of chalky ground
black ravens and bedraggled white seagulls hop broken-winged
and a mute wind clangs jagged tons of metal

here from dark murky worlds of blood and blindness
here where the air breaths thick with rotting dreams
in rasping tones of hatred that echo our voices
comes a plaintive, pervasive, insistent whispering

"we are the dangerous blessings
we are jagged, we are flabby
we are inflamed oozing sores
we are a bright-eyed boy's cancerous tumor
we are the fear and hatred that pulls the trigger
we are diabetes, bombs, nausea, vomit, boredom, greed
we are the bicycle tumble, head hit, last breath in the street
death of a frizzy headed young woman

we are separation and calamity
we are the outline of the space of each living cell
we are the rind of the orange, the shell of the peanut
the itchy, flaking, dead top layer of your skin

we are the dangerous blessings
and we are falling weak-kneed lonely for your embrace
we yearn for your premonition, your memory
we listen avidly to hear you
speak our names without rancor or disgust
we beg ragged and hungry
for any tiny glance of accepting friendliness

we are the dangerous blessings
we too are the whisper of the divine
we are the blessings of the god
whom you believe has forsaken you
and we are kin to the blessing of the first breath
of a rosy juicy human infant

infinite as stars ponderous as tears
we whisper our anguished call

beyond the vast blue ocean of adventure and peril
beyond the silver bolts of the grand electric city on the hill
beyond the earth packed village with glowing fire at the hearth
beyond the junkyard where we huddle with our shame
beyond all stories, wishes, happenings and imaginings
on a home street of shared purpose
in a clean wooden wagon
joy with pigtails pulls sobbing despair
for we are all playmates
we are all blessings
we exist"

Blessed Be The Transformation Of Energy

Blessed Be The Transformation Of Energy
Blessed Be The Transformation Of Energy
Blessed Be The Transformation Of Energy
Blessed Be The Transformation Of Energy
Blessed Be The Transformation Of Energy
Blessed Be The Transformation Of Energy
Blessed Be The Transformation Of Energy
Blessed Be The Transformation Of Energy
Blessed Be The Transformation Of Energy
Blessed Be The Transformation Of Energy
Blessed Be The Transformation Of Energy
Blessed Be The Transformation Of Energy
Blessed Be The Transformation Of Energy
Blessed Be The Transformation Of Energy
Blessed Be The Transformation Of Energy
Blessed Be The Transformation Of Energy
Blessed Be The Transformation Of Energy
Blessed Be The Transformation Of Energy
Blessed Be The Transformation Of Energy
Blessed Be The Transformation Of Energy
Blessed Be The Transformation Of Energy
Blessed Be The Transformation Of Energy
Blessed Be The Transformation Of Energy
Blessed Be The Transformation Of Energy
Blessed Be The Transformation Of Energy
Blessed Be The Transformation Of Energy

Illumination

It's love that binds the atoms
Love that knits the bone
It's love that rots all flesh
And love that erodes stone

In love's sweet embrace of freedom
An intimate moment is born
In which laughter cries "Awake"
And desire's grip from self is torn

It's love that beats the heart
Love that takes each breath
It's love that breaks all form apart
And love that comes as death

On This Day

I offer you sweet space
An empty gift
A passionate devotion
An attraction to the color of your hair
An addiction to the timbre of your voice
A gleeful anticipation of your smile
These are the wrappings
The true gift
I offer freely
It is nothing
And you are not obligated
Either to accept, refuse or even notice
This silent space
Uncontained by love.

The Earth Endures

The earth endures
She shall rejoice
She shall joy
In the love of her lovers

The Earth Endures

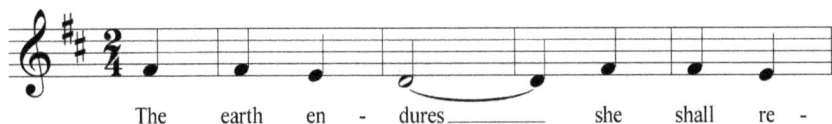

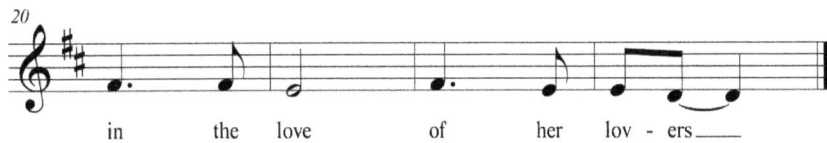

The earth en - dures_____ she shall re -

joice she shall joy in the love

of her lov - ers_____ The eath en - dures_____

_____ she shall re - joice she shall joy

in the love of her lov - ers_____

Writes Itself

this poem writes itself in water
laces sunlight through green branches
vein-patterns into thought
and past thought
into comfortable blue sky truth
recites in leaf flutter
chances in innocence
that i may overhear the sound
of this ordinary grass growing afternoon
this poem tickles itself in breezes
rollicks in yellow wildflower abandon
pleased that i stand still
on the brown earth
sensing the water within
satisfied that i stand animal-eared alert

She Is Here With Us

in the wild shimmer of the afternoon
our friendship a perfect reflection
of the curve and shake of the redwood branch
each of us content chat and amble along a dirt road

as the wind blows through our minds
mouthing emptiness wide eyed
sun ray and shadow dappled
we stand together in the essential light

and she is here with us

with a slow shiver of descending needles
with a dusty ground spiral rising
with a sparkle of bird song
wind blown leaf strewn
infused with the aroma of spores and moss
touched by the generous sky of the afternoon
with the earth underfoot

she is here with us

This Rainy Morning

The poem I hear this rainy morning
is wild
not responsive to my gentle query
nor to the familiar rustle of fresh pages
turning in my journal.

This morning
I don't want to wrest control from the torrent
or tame words of desolation.

I want a lamp, a phone call
and cereal warm with nurturance now.

Outside my window
a growling whinny, snapping branches and shadow flashes
whirl in wetness.

The poem
as translucent as water
pounds down the soil, muddies my mind
and beats a persistent invitation
to wash clean of comfort.

With no warning
the rain stops.

As the wind waits
I find myself still looking out the window
where in stillness now
neither loss nor possibility
obscure my view of freedom.

Suddenly

This soft blue afternoon
Strikes like lightening.
In agonizing orgasm,
I am blinked awake
To no image in the infinite mirror.

Rain In Summer

rain falls in summer like sheets
                              hanging as walls
between dank earth cellars   and memories of sunshine
        brain in brittle decay   no memory of bath
                        no morning haircut
sheets shadow like early dusk   no memory of leaf falling
                no memory of bowel stains
        body rain of wrinkles   jowls hanging sheets of skin
                balding groin and ruined left knee
we sit in your living room
                        surrounded by paintings signed with your name
        we draw a picture   each of us   we take turns
"i'm sorry, you cannot shampoo your hair alone,
                because you may forget to turn off the water,
        or rinse out the soap"   i answer you
                        we draw portraits of each other
                        with pencil
                in a soft and tiny pad of paper
        you frown at me
                        annoyed at how stupid I can be
about soap and water and doing it yourself
                                you ask "who drew this?"
        i thank you for asking   i tell you that you drew it
                i speak of bravery
        billowing like sheets   hanging as walls
between dark crumbling fungus smells
                and memories of summer fresh laundry
                still hanging in the sun

while thoughts   like sheets fallen under the summer rain
                    into the dirt
        all crumpled   mud stained   splotched
                    moldy and ragged
            fall like rain between personality and mind
        like a page turning
                        between my sketch of you
                    and your drawing of me
                no memory of loss
                no memory of now

Signposts I Have Seen Along The Road

just regular years
no significant
star spangled decade
a slow gray tar two lane road
wizened bushes
with small whitish flowers
tobacco ads, shaving cream
one word
on each precarious stick

i am a bit player
i thought i was the star
trying to fit into my skin
you
walk in the screen door
i'm coming out
our eyes recognize
we mutter "hi"
to an unknown hope

thirsty?
hungry?
your
dream
will
come
true
in
one
mile

the store blinks glare
inside and out
give and get
money, cigarettes, beer, hair gel
these years
mark my dusty road to death
caught up
in the story of themselves

Signposts I Have Found In The General Jumble

Silence

Stillness

Spaciousness

Serenity

Good Morning

At 7:30 this morning, while I am pulling on my black cotton sock with the small hole in the heel, strategy and integrity confront each other in my stomach.

Strategy is a con man with a big shiny smile, an aikido expert with a sword, a whirling dervish of spiritual ascension.

Integrity, as poor as a beggar too drunk to ask, as supple as a willow branch, dull like bits of invisible dust on city streets, is interested in surrender and tempted to die.

In a contraction of the events of my life, they meet, they clash.

In the haste of his expertise the dervish trips over the semiconscious soul.

Once again, the smile has ignored the grime.

The branch and the sword execute perfectly the choreography of an ancient dance of survival.

I, spellbound by the show but revived by humility, put on my other sock.

At 7:32 in the morning I slip into my shoes, stand, stretch and sigh into an expansive and inevitable willingness to breakfast with them both.

The Dying Club

I have an announcement today about your free membership in
the dying club. This is not a tricky offer, not an empty
promise, there are no secret charges. This is a real and
meaningful association that you, simply by being born, have
earned the unique and yet universal opportunity to participate
in to your fullest ability. There are no dues, no minutes, no
meetings, no rules, you are welcome as you are. No exclusions,
permissions, requirements of age, sex, race, nationality,
political bias, religion, health conditions, crimes,
accomplishments, acceptance or defiance changes your mem-
bership status. If you have ever felt inadequate, excluded,
persecuted, ugly, superior, blessed, knowledgeable, rightous or
beautiful, don't worry we are all equal members in the dying
club. There is no dress code, no board of directors, no statute
of limitations, no special qualification or accommodation at all,
ever. You are, actually, already a member. There is nothing you
have to complete, send back, answer, no card to carry, there is
nothing you can do that would cause expulsion. I am simply
reminding you and myself that we are each free and equal
lifetime members of the dying club.

Time

time wakes me every morning
introduces itself anew ageless, beautiful
infinitely cheerful.
time has no understanding
of hesitation or regret.
time is unbiased
flexible in mind and body
a good companion in any endeavor
as long as you are not in a hurry.

time can be secretive
but not in a mean way
it's just that it
may begin a game of consequence
without having asked beforehand
whether you want to participate.
if there is a disagreement
time becomes extremely competitive
and always strives to win.
though time can be self effacing and pleasant
it is not capable of compromise or generosity.

because time does not lower its' standards
or accommodate for changing situations
it can appear harsh and uncaring.
but time is truly loyal non-judgmental
peaceful in crisis and fun in adventure.
time accepts me exactly as i am
and makes no demands
except that i recognize and acknowledge its' presence.

All My Stuff Talks To Each Other
Window To Trim

Window: "You are not tight enough!"

Trim: "I do my best."

Window: "It's the influence of house. You are intimidated by house and you ignore me."

Trim: "Ah, come on!"

Window: "It's true. House pulls you away. You look right through me."

Trim: "I thought you liked that."

Window: "What I like, I like you to fit tight."

House: "You both drive me nuts."

Trim: "I do my best!"

Window: "Well, it's not good enough, I'm so upset, I'm shaking to pieces. I'm loose, I'm drafty. I need you.."

Trim: "I'm so sorry."

House: "Trim, never mind, I'm with you for the long haul, come on, we can always get a new window."

Window: "I need you!"

Trim: "I'm confused, I have strong feelings for both of you, but I have to take care of myself. I can't just fall out of the wall to take care of you."

All My Stuff Talks To Each Other
Floorboard To Floorboard And Me

Grade C: "You don't like me because I'm so colorful and inteesting."
Me: "I don't like you because you are so brash and mixed up."
Grade C: "People admire my interesting patterning all the time."
Me: "They don't see the difference between your streaks and shadows and dirt."
Grade A to Grade C: "Don't worry about it, nobody notices her enough to listen."

All My Stuff Talks To Each Other

The Dish Ran Away With The Spoon

Cup: "Why didn't you stay home with me?"

Spoon: "You always wanted me to stir things and you only wanted me to stir things up and I just wanted to be, you know, relaxed together."

Cup: "And now?"

Spoon: "Well, now, you know, I survived, and dish is broken, so, here I am."

Cup: "I missed you. Let's saucer...."

All My Stuff Talks To Each Other
Teapot to Teapot

"You're hot!"
"You're not."
"Cinnamon spice"
"Left over green"
"No caffeine in our cupboard!"
"I know what you mean"
"I have an up spout"
"I have a down"
"Do you drip when you pour?"
"No, I'm fine when I serve
You have a nerve!"
"No! I have a drip
I was trying to solve
Thought you might have a tip!"
"Oh, okay then, see you at tea"
"Yes, hey, you're still hot
I like you a lot"

I Am No Longer Who I Am

I am no longer who I am
my name is not my name
still it's true
if in thought or word or deed
I act unkindly to you
then I feel the pain

I am no longer who I am
my name is not my name
still it's true
if in thought or word or deed
I act kindly to you
then I feel the joy

I am no longer who I am
my name is not my name
still it's true
I am that I am
and my name is you

I Am No Longer Who I Am

I am no lon-ger who I am, my name is not my name,

still it's true if in thought or word or deed I act un-kind-ly to

you then I___ feel the pain. I am no lon-ger

who I am my name is not my name, still it's true

if in thought ir word or deed I act kindl-ly to you

then I___ feel the joy. I am no lon-ger who I am, my

name is not my name, still it's true I am that I am and my

name is you.

Benediction

This is the color of my soul
green glistening, wet with pain
orange ember, dry with joy.
This is the story of my soul
a tiny black stone,
a heave of smoke,
filaments of opalescence
like rays of light.
This is the center of the black stone
a geode surprise of space,
a diamond heart buried in the
hardness of life.
This is the ray of light
and where it falls
a benediction beyond doubt
that I can love anyone
as I love you.

Emptiness Like A Jar Full Of Life

embodied by glass
smooth solid like stone
embodied by skin
live veined as a leaf
a glass jar and i
each whole and breakable
yet empty in emptiness
so very nothing
slowly my hand
slides the jar
to the edge of a table
suddenly a breeze flutters me

Hungry Ghost

I'm a tiger ready to spring
I'm a tiger after my prey
I'm a baby ready to play
I'm a baby, I'm wild with wonder
I'm a tiger, it's my nature to kill
I'm a tiger, I want to eat my fill
I'm a baby, I'm hungry for everything I see
I'm a baby, I grab what I will

I am your lover, I'm your mama, I am your friend
I love your twinkle, I care for your mind
I touch softly your skin, I bandage your wounds,
I clean your bottom, I cook your food
I give you money
I give you apples and honey
I love you
I love you so much
I could eat you up

Really, I'm a human being
Really, just like you
I walk around
I don't have to pretend to be real
Really, I love you
Really, I want you
It's what I feel

I'm a hungry ghost
I'm a hungry ghost
Whatever comes near me
That's what I want most
I try to take what I want
I grab what I can
I want your love
I want you
I want to be happy
I want to be full
I want you to be happy and gleeful and fun
I'm a human being
I'm all and I'm one

I'm like a tiger ready to spring
I'm like a baby ready to play
I'm like a baby I want what I want
I'm like a tiger wild with desire
I'm a hungry ghost
I love you so much
I could eat you up

Another Birthday

another birthday,
another sunrise,
love repeats itself
in an infinite loop of delight.
i love you today
just as i did yesterday.
this same love
rests in the night
and rises each morning
in subtle shininess,
almost invisible.
tomorrow
after, when we die,
birds wings
will still pattern the shininess,
and someone else
will write a poem
for another birthday.

Toot-Toot

whatever toots your horn
whets your whistle
sings your song

A full blown rose is not an orange poppy.
For sure, your lover is not my lover.
That curly headed human
peddling the red tricycle
was in your particular womb,
and the dark eyed one
lying in the shaded grass
was in mine.
A ginger snap is not a chocolate chip.

whatever catches your eye
rings your bell
tolls your days

Whatever you need
to satiate your particular
universal hunger.

Silly

Here is a poem by Rumi
                    he gives me a candle
                    to walk up a dark staircase
Here is Oliver
              she watches a robin red breast
              swoop and gently land on my hand
Yeats
    places a small square all white puzzle by my bedside
    I am meant to find it when I wake up

Here is a poem by me
                  it doesn't have any words
                  the whole poem is hidden in spaces
                  that are not even there
                  completely unintelligible
                  written especially for you
                  here is a flock of geese pointing the way
                  obviously this poem has nothing to say
                  yet it is so lyrical
                  I laugh as I sing it to you
                  my feet hop dance to the right
                  backwards and to the left
                  I cannot stop laughing
                  as I sing and dance this poem to you

Here is Lorca
   adding the secret music of the spheres
And cummings
    tells me that I absolutely must
        put in
        the word
        LOVE

One Word At A Time

One Word
In the Beginning
Was The Word.
What Word was it?

One Word

leads to another
a promise unlocked
already dead
just from being opened

One Word

lying dry inked
on the white page
one word is enough
but not enough
to explain its own meaning

One Word At A Time

One Word
loneliness
a word that stands alone

Proliferation
This is called
Thought
Don't believe it
For a minute

One Word
poetry like wildflowers
fragile, quick to die
I lose interest
if one word
is mushy, broken, too loose, too tight
not orange blossomed

Poetry Book

.........it's a good thing poetry books are slim
too much, too thick, too true
i'm outta here, what about you?

Blessed Be

The Transformation

Of Energy

www.ingramcontent.com/pod-product-compliance
Lightning Source LLC
Chambersburg PA
CBHW060159070426
42447CB00033B/2217